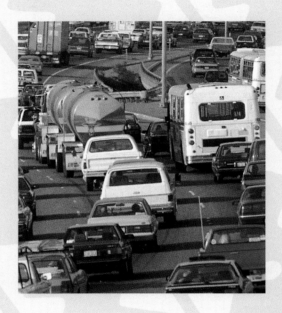

Lisa Trumbauer

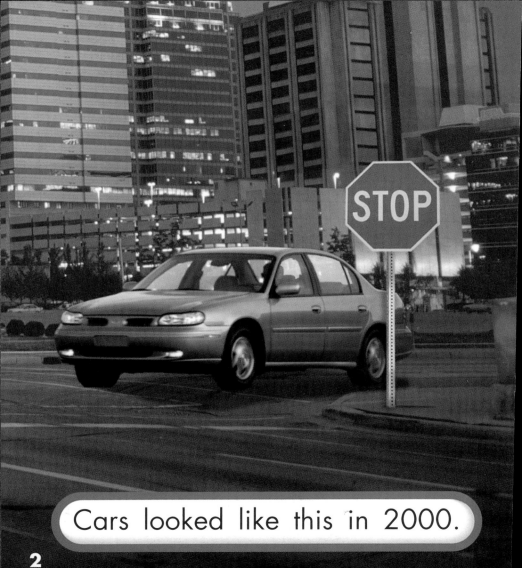

Cars looked like this in 2000.

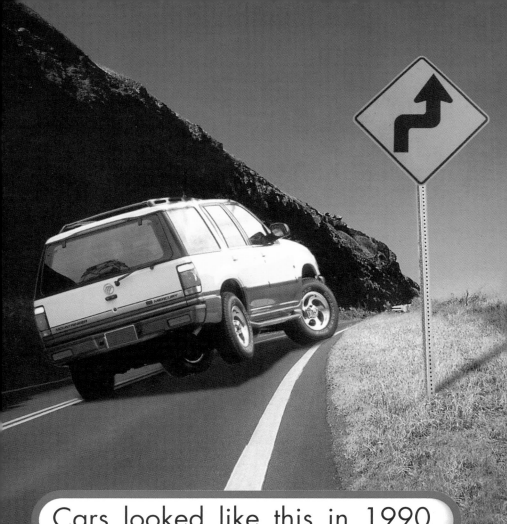

Cars looked like this in 1990.

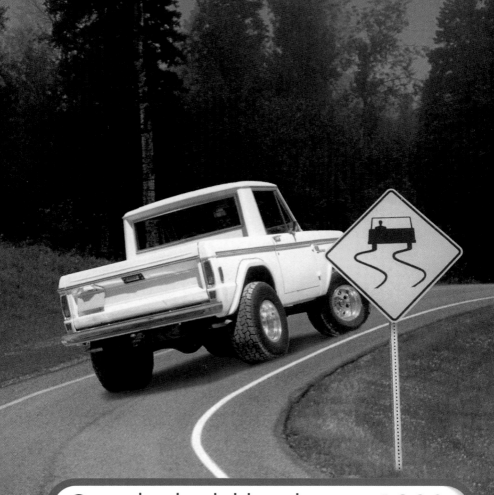

Cars looked like this in 1980.

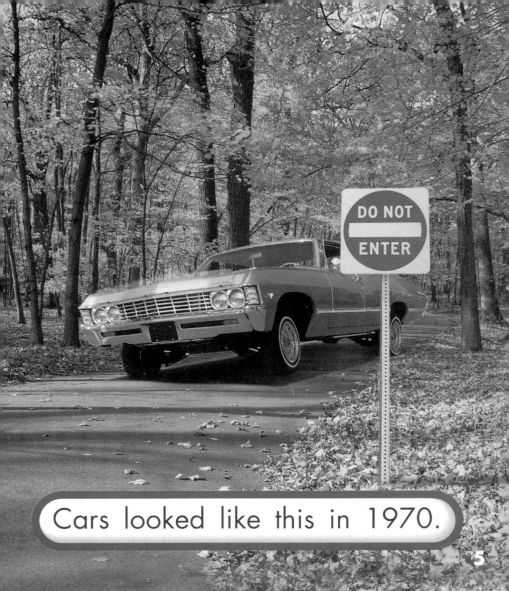

Cars looked like this in 1970.

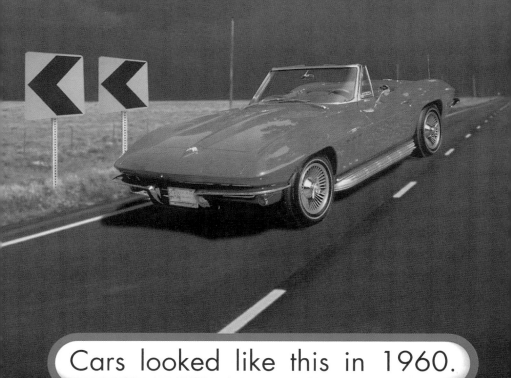

Cars looked like this in 1960.

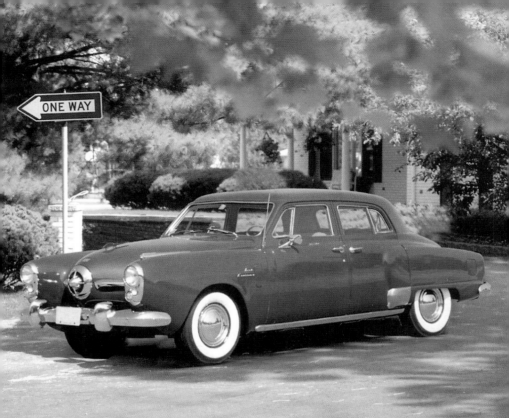

Cars looked like this in 1950.

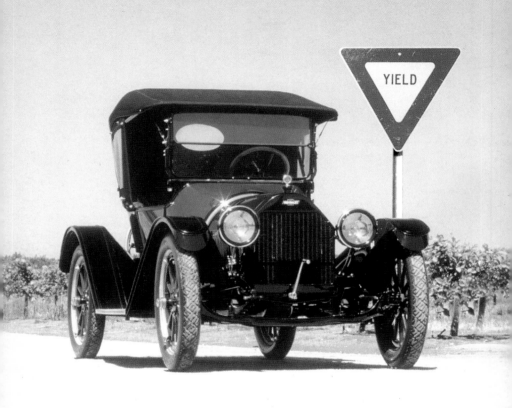

This is a really old car!